MASTER DATING ONLINE

One Man's Journey To Find Love On The Internet

By

Chris Masters

Looking for other books and projects by this author? Visit chrismastersbooks.com for updates and free stuff!

Contents

Chapter 1: Great Expectations

My dating life may have been hampered by my Catholic upbringing. I never discussed intimate relationships in detail with my parents when I was growing up. Instead, my parents gave me and my brothers a set of books to read that explained everything we needed to know about sex, as told from the Vatican's perspective. I'm sure the Pope had my best interests in mind when he wrote a 4 volume set on sex education. However, my older brother was the first to get "the books" and held onto them for the good part of 20 years. Maybe he was a slow reader, or just liked the detailed pictures. By the time I got to look at them I think the information was no longer relevant. "Vagina" was called a "Vestibule", and "Penis" was "The Holy Staff of Ra".

I muddled through the dating world as I entered college and into my employment years. During that time I believed I would find the woman of my dreams, settle down in a house in suburbia, have 2-3 kids and a couple of pets, and join the group called "grown ups." There had to be someone out there especially for me. That's what all the Hallmark commercials led me to believe. Being the studious person that I am, I took classes on dating, bought books on dating, even hired a dating coach. She prepped me by selecting my wardrobe, teaching me how to cook and pick out wine, and how to discuss my inner feelings. Still, I had limited luck. I felt skilled but not confident, and just a little awkward asking women out on dates. After years of dating, attending dating classes, having friends set me up on dates, and spending hours and thousands of dollars on meals, coffee, flowers, gifts, and the like, I finally decided this was not the best way to spend my time. I turned to online dating as a way to cut through the blind selection methods, finding women who had the same interests and values. It seemed like a miracle to find women who matched my desires and fit well with my personality, all with just a few keystrokes. Not everyone was a match, but there was hope as I improved I would locate a more suitable partner.

Why did I write this book?

My goal is to leave you with a little more knowledge about the online dating world while entertaining you in the process. Dating in the 21st century is a daunting task. Most people are hit with information from all sides. Dating sites are unfair to both men and women. Women are slammed with emails, primarily from guys who have little interest in delving beyond their profile pictures. Communication skills and basic manners were thrown out the Windows as well, with most email exchanges from men to women being only one or two words and pictures of unmentionable body parts. Overly confident men send pictures of their penis to show women they too have read the Vatican's books on sex. Unfortunately, like my brother, they only focused on the pictures. This gives many women the opportunity to look at the male genitalia and wonder which head these men are thinking with when sending email. I never saw the point of photographing a part of my body and sending it to a woman to demonstrate my size. Guys, if you truly want to impress her, have the Eiffel Tower displayed in the background for comparison purposes.

Men are at a major disadvantage when looking for a mate online because of the sheer numbers. When online dating began, there were 50 or more men to every 1 woman on the Internet. While the percentage has evened out over the years, men initiate the most contact leaving women pages of emails to read and reply. To prevent female members from running away screaming, dating sites use filters and ways to block contact so answering mail is manageable. This great feature helps women but frustrates men because guys never know if their email has been read or flushed down the Internet toilet.

Most people learn by example, and I hope you'll learn something from my life experiences. It's that old adage of, "give a man a fish and he'll eat for a day, but teach a man to fish and he'll make sushi." Lucky for you, by reading this book, you won't have the same online dates I had to endure. It's tough to meet people, especially with the many demands we all face on a daily basis. If you're not part of a social group or feel uncomfortable dating members of your church, and you want to make the best of online dating, then read on.

Is there someone on the Internet for me?

The answer to that question is a resounding...maybe. Just as with any dating service, the quality of the members and the ability to find someone who meets your wants and needs will differ. You may live in an area where there are many members, but the website doesn't put much effort into screening every Tom, Dick, and Dick, and Dick, and well, you know. Or you could live in an area where the selection is small and from good quality stock, but you don't want to date your 2nd cousin, AGAIN. Do you?

Some websites guarantee you will find your 'true love', even if you live in Bugscuffle, Tennessee. It's up to you to make a major life decision to journey to some far off land to find true love. I argue that there is someone probably closer with similar personality traits, and you don't need to pack a suitcase just to meet for coffee.

What if my true love lives in Bugscuffle, Tennessee?

They just might. I'm not here to discourage you from diving into the deep end of the date pool to meet a few potential kissing fish. You might find the love of your life on one of the many dating websites. It's up to you to take the plunge and search. But what you learn from my adventures might save you a lot of time and aggravation.

This book is a humorous compilation of the people and encounters I had while looking for someone compatible over the Internet. Not every date I had was a disaster. I met many wonderful women on Internet dating sites. But nobody wants to hear about the good times. Nobody. The stories you're about to read are my absolute worst dates. Names in this book were changed for obvious reasons. If, as you're reading this book, you come across a character that describes someone you know perfectly, insert their name and continue reading to make it even more enjoyable.

My experience in writing a book on Internet dating has been interesting too.

You would think writing a humorous book about Internet dating would be easy. Au contraire! As I penned the first line:

"In these hallowed pages lie stories of sirens and seductresses, hags and harlots, erotic tales of bliss and happenstance..."

The legal department of Cohen, Cohen, and Kahn sent me a memo claiming that under no uncertain terms can I call the women I dated "sirens and seductresses". Primarily because the attorneys thought this was false advertising. Later the same day I received a parchment scroll from Local Witches Guild 1877 in Sacramento stating they would turn me into a public toilet seat if I didn't take out the word "hags". Oh, and to top it all off, most respectable publishers won't touch any manuscript with words like "harlots" and "erotic tales of bliss."

This leaves me with: "In these hallowed pages lie stories of happenstance."

That is what you'll find here, hallowed pages or not.

Many thanks go out to Kim Evans for giving me the push to write this book and to her, Helen Bradley, and Susan Earl for their review and editing skills. Also kudos to my parents for enduring my many rants and calls of frustration in my years of trying to understand relationships.

Chapter 2: The Taming of the Shrew

I was an early user of Match.com when it debuted in 1995. Being in the group of the first 21,000 members, I was probably one of the original men who signed up in Savannah, Georgia. There weren't really any rules for online dating then. Most profiles only gave the basics of what you and your possible match liked and didn't like. You sent them an email and if the person liked what you wrote, you would exchange phone numbers and set up a date.

Today, most people would advise you to meet your date in a public place, require three forms of valid ID, and have them strip searched by an off duty police officer. Since computer dating was so new back then, it was common for the guy to meet his date at her front door and actually take her someplace. Other than going directly to her house, there were few places to meet besides the mall, a bar, or restaurant. It would be another six years before Starbucks came to town, and I doubt any woman would have waited that long for a decaf latte.

This was my first online to offline date, and I wanted to make a great first impression. At the time I was the proud owner of a new, brightly polished red Mazda pickup truck. I relished the new car smell as I watched the reflection of the setting sun on the shiny cherry red hood. In the South, a pickup truck has one of three uses. First and foremost it can be a utility vehicle, hauling stuff from one place to another. Some trucks are mud-bogging machines, jacked up higher than a giraffe's ass and caked from bumper to bumper in many layers of dirt. Only the smallest percentage of trucks are kept pristine, used more for show and deluxe transportation than utility. Ask any puritan truck owner to haul a load of dirt and they'll either refuse your request or spend twelve hours washing off every speck of dust afterwards. I was THAT guy.

I parked on the street outside my date's home and strolled up to the door. I was nervous because I really didn't know that much about this woman. Yes, we did email back and forth and I talked with her briefly over the phone to secure a date. Beyond that, I wanted to get to know her face-to-face to see her reaction and know if we were a good fit. After ringing the doorbell I stood patiently, waiting for an answer. In a nearby window I saw a curtain being pushed aside by a cat eyeing me from the ledge of a table. If all else fails, I thought, at least we can talk about her cat.

The door popped open and I was greeted by a short woman with dirty blond hair wearing a gray sweatsuit. Whoa. This wasn't my date, I hoped. She looked up at me and said, "who are you?"

Feeling like a door-to-door salesman, I made my pitch.

"Hello. I'm Chris, and I'm here to take Melissa out on a date." I said, not really ready to speak to a gatekeeper. Could this be a roommate? Sister? Wrong address? God, I hope I'm not being filmed for an episode of Punk'd/America's Funniest Home Videos/Candid Camera.

"Wait right here." She closed the door abruptly and I could hear her talking in the hallway. Great. Most women don't let unfamiliar men in the house for security reasons. Unlike most guys who don't let anyone in the house because they don't want to be reported to the health department.

A few minutes later, Melissa showed up at the front door. "Hello," she said, "I see you made it." Her long, wavy, almond colored hair was still damp from the shower. She was wearing a flowery purple dress and a pair of white sandals. I was relieved to see she matched her photo, but her tone of voice left me unsure if she really wanted to go out.

"Of course I made it. Did you think I wouldn't?" She looked as though I had caught her in the middle of something. "Are you ready to go?" I asked, thinking maybe it was too early to meet for a date. We'd agreed on the time, or I thought we had agreed.

She was very pretty and only a few years older than me. Based on our profiles we had many things in common, so I was looking forward to learning more about her.

Peering around me, she took one look at my truck and whined, "are we going in... that?" Her expression changed from curious wonder to serious disappointment. I stared back at her in disbelief. "I don't like trucks" she told me, "they're dirty."
"As you can see," I pointed to the shininess of the newly waxed finish and the clean and fresh interior, "there is no dirt touching this truck."

She wrinkled her nose and shook her head as she walked to the passenger side. Being the gentleman that I am, I opened the door and waited for her to get in. She paused for a moment, assessed the truck interior, and carefully slid inside. We talked casually on the way to the restaurant, but I sensed she was not impressed with my mode of transportation.
Her profile had raved about how much she loved Mexican food,

so I took her to the best Mexican restaurant I could find in Savannah. It was affordable and the food was good.

"Why here?" She said, slightly irritated. What now? Was she hoping for a five star restaurant?

"Your profile said Mexican food was your favorite." I said, feeling rather queasy.

"Oh, I had to put something down to fill out my profile. Nobody seems to read them anyway. This is fine. We can eat here."

The restaurant had the typical ethnic Latin flare: clay figurines from Mexico, sombreros hanging on the walls like cheap art, stucco textured pillars with a fake trellis, and prickly cacti in brightly painted pots. We were seated at a large wooden table facing a colorful handmade rug stapled to the wall next to an illuminated Corona sign. The dinner crowd was increasing. We were lucky to get a table before a line started forming out the door. Sounds of various conversations and the clanking of utensils on plates filled the air.

By now, I wasn't feeling much love coming from the other side of the table. Maybe we just started out a little bumpy and the rest of the date would go smoother. I ordered some nachos as an excuse to talk less. "Make sure they're fresh," she directed the waiter, "I hate when I get stale chips."

Sensing the tension, the waiter quickly brought us our appetizer, and I reached for the jalapeno pepper sitting on the plate. "Maybe we could play a round." I said and Melissa looked at me quizzically. I pointed to the television hanging over the bar behind her head. A golf tournament was being televised. She glanced at the TV, turned back to me and said, "I don't play golf. I only put that in my profile because rich guys play golf."

I could feel myself squirming in the chair. Not good. In less than 30 minutes I'd been insulted, humiliated, and deceived. How long was this date going to last? I found myself praying for divine intervention. If I can make it through dinner I'll just take her home. That's all. We will part ways and I won't have to see her again. I mean, what else could happen?

22

Lucky me. Karma stepped in to save the day. When I bit into the juicy jalapeno pepper, caustic juice squirted out. I watched in disbelief as a fine stream of acid cleared the top of her menu and landed smack dab in the middle of her left eye. If I'd tried to replicate that move a million times I could never make it happen again. It was a very unfortunate bullseye. Screaming ensued.

"AAAAAAAAAaaaaaAAAAAaaaaaAAAAAAAAAAAHHHHHHHH " She shrieked as the waiter helped flush her eye with a pitcher of water. Her screams caused a hush to fall over the restaurant. Even a baby two tables away stopped crying, wondering what the commotion was all about. The manager came running over to help, bringing towels from the kitchen to mop up the water now covering the table and floor. The more the situation escalated, the harder she cried "Take me home NOW!!!"

I paid the check and we quickly made it to the door. With her hand on my shoulder, I guided her out of the restaurant to prevent her from tripping over the other patrons. She blindly staggered out, makeup running halfway down her face, smeared mascara, a swollen eyelid, and her dress drenched with water and tears. I was sure everyone standing in the line outside the restaurant thought I'd been smacking her around with a fajita pan. As we passed through the crowd, men pushed their wide-eyed wives/girlfriends behind them, shielding them from whatever attacked my date. I'm sure a few people never went inside, thinking this restaurant was just a little too spicy for their taste.

Needless to say, the ride home was very quiet. She did her best not to look at me with her bright red eye. As I rolled up to her house, I turned to her and said, "I'm so sor…"

"STOP! Just stop right here!" she squealed, cutting me off mid sentence. She threw open the truck door, slammed it hard (oh my baby!), and stomped quickly into her house. I drove away tired and hungry.

It would be a long time before I wanted Mexican food again.

Chapter 3: The Time Machine

Given the opportunity to go back in time, I would. There are people who claim the 'butterfly effect' would ruin the future. In essence if you change just one thing on our path, even altering the course of a butterfly's flight, it would make ripples that affect everything in the span of time. But I argue there are moments in our lives we would be better off never enduring in the first place. Some experiences didn't make me stronger or more likely to change the path I was on, they just caused years of nightmares afterwards.

This was one of those occasions.

As I watched online dating sites improve over the years, I witnessed a number of ways to connect with other members. Email was the first way to interact, followed by chat rooms. Chat rooms offered a quick way to communicate and get to know a prospective date faster than email. This had an added benefit for women because other people helped monitor group conversation. Anyone acting inappropriately would be kicked from chat by the moderator. When instant messaging was added, it gave guys three ways to bombard women. They were swamped with loads of emails, propositioned in chat rooms, and showered with instant messaging requests. Since there were twenty guys to every girl online, it was a literal feeding frenzy.

One morning I was hanging out in a chat room, discussing the finer points of restaurants in my town. As is customary, members would say 'hi' to your screen name as you entered chat. Most guys are quick to welcome women, but shy away if the conversation gets too detailed. I noticed a woman from my state enter the chat room, so I reached out to her first.

She seemed like a sweet, country girl. We chatted about her life, and what she wanted to accomplish. "Nothing really, I just live a simple life," she typed.

The only activity she said she loved was sitting for hours on end, making jewelry at home.

After a few emails, she sent me her picture. I was surprised she looked younger than her age. She had long brown hair, emerald green eyes, and a vibrant smile sandwiched between two dimpled cheeks. Behind her in the picture was a rusty old tractor. Her thin frame was dwarfed by a massive tractor tire. She stood defiant leaning forward with her foot on the inside of the tire as if she had the power to push the heap of metal uphill. I wondered why such a cute girl wasn't being asked out often. She told me she lived "out in the sticks" and had few neighbors nearby.

We exchanged phone numbers and set up a date to meet. She raved about a restaurant she loved, so I agreed to meet her there for lunch.

The address she gave me didn't show up on the map, but I knew it was between two towns, so I headed off on a journey to find it. I'll never do that again. I left with 30 minutes to spare only to find the place five minutes before the date. I had spent two hours driving through dirt roads and detouring around closed streets.

When I passed a burned out mobile home with a used car graveyard, I was ready to give up. Then I came upon a old red barn with a weathered sign dangling from two rusty chains that read "Bobby's Good Eats." The parking lot was full of rusted cars and trucks. A full parking lot is usually the sign of a good restaurant. Wait. The small print at the bottom of the sign read, "NO FOOD FOR 50 MILES IN ANY DIRECTION."

Stressed about the drive and the impending date made my heart beat faster. What the hell am I doing out here? This place is in the middle of nowhere. I'm sure that everyone here was friendly. Suddenly I stopped in my tracks and ducked. Less than a mile away I heard the crack of several gunshots followed by the Southern victory cry "YEEEEEE-HAWWWWWW".

I turned in the direction of the shots, and a ragged old man poked his head out of one of the many rusty, beat-up trucks in the parking lot. He was wearing a dirty pair of overalls, with no shirt. Wisps of grey hair floated around his head. "Sounds like he got 'em one."

"One what?" I replied to him, not really trying to engage in conversation.

"Somethin' that was alive an kickin', I gay-ess." He smiled revealing three teeth remaining on his upper jaw, and a cheek full of chewing tobacco discoloring what was left of his bottom row. His attention turned to me. "Say, mister, you interested in some 'shine? Ten dollars a quart."

I shuffled two steps forward to peer into his truck bed. Several sizes of mason jars were neatly arranged in red plastic crates. The jars were filled with clear liquid and smelled like paint thinner, even from a distance. I glanced at him, looked at the jars, then back up at him, and shook my head no.

He looked me up and down and focused on my clean appearance and neatly pressed clothes, "Ya got outta church? Why ya goin' to church on Saturday?"

He laughed a bit. Then his laugh turned into a cough. At that point I realized he was smoking near the shine. Since I didn't want to be blown to pieces, my pace quickened as I made a beeline to the restaurant/barn/redneck Civic Center.

The interior could be best described as "countrified." This is where the original concept of nailing artifacts to restaurant walls started. Some backwoods Picasso went postal in this place. Hundreds of nails impaled farm implements, old rusted signs, and antique pictures of people standing in front of log cabins and canvas tents. A mural size Confederate flag hung prominently on the far wall with a framed sign saying "We Will Never Forget!"

Lovely. In the background I swear I could hear a banjo playing...

Many busboys and waitresses walked through a lobby that was a bridge between the kitchen and main hall. A party of twelve people were having a birthday celebration, so I squeezed past them to find an open seat at the far end of the lobby. Once the crowd thinned, I saw a woman standing next to the entrance looking in my direction. She was small in stature, but round in shape. Her brownish-grey hair was pulled tightly behind her head, slightly elevating her eyebrows, and making her look a little surprised. Her body was draped in a flowery moo-moo and her dusty feet hung over well worn leather sandals. I diverted my eyes to the picture I'd printed out from my computer then glanced back at her. She caught my glance and smiled, showing a bright set of teeth, minus a few, sandwiched between two dimpled cheeks. The only difference between the picture in my hands and the woman standing in front of me was 20 more years and 150 additional pounds. Nope, it couldn't be her. I locked my eyes on the picture, pondering any possible positive outcomes.

"Hello" I heard a feeble voice directed to me.

I was dazed. When I looked up two seconds later she made her way to me without a sound. My heart sank as I realized this must be my date.

"Hello. Are you...Nancy?" I said, braced for bad news. Considering the off-road drive, the gunfire, the creepy moonshine salesman, and the largest Confederate flag ever made, this seemed like the natural progression of my day.

"Yes", she said as her eyes glanced at me then fell to her shoes.

For a moment I wondered what I was supposed to do. This obviously wasn't the woman I was expecting. Now what? I was hungry, and drove this entire way, so at least I should have a meal and figure out what to do.

My thoughts were interrupted by a bubbly waitress who greeted us both, "How y'all doin' today? Two for lunch?"

We were seated near the center of the restaurant in an area that had much larger chairs. When the waitress brought us drinks, I told Nancy she didn't look much like her photo. She blushed and shied away from an explanation. I didn't know if this was a joke or she thought I would somehow overlook this glaring error.

I ordered a club sandwich, and she ordered...a side salad. That was all. I guessed her stomach was probably in knots. She was chatty online, but with me a few feet away, not so much.

After we finished eating, another waitress came up to our table. "Hello Rita," she said, "good to see you back after the breakfast buffet."

Well now. That's an interesting side note. I asked her, "If you're Rita, who's Nancy?"

She cleared her throat and spoke quietly, "Nancy is my daughter. I sent you her picture because everyone says I look just like her."

I noticed a slight resemblance, but couldn't believe what I was hearing.

"I didn't think we would ever meet since it's only on the computer." She stared at her half eaten salad,"what's on the computer ain't real."

I almost choked, "You're right. Some things AREN'T real on the computer. But we talked on the phone! I sent you a picture! I'm sitting here, in this barn, having lunch with you right now!" I was a little annoyed, but more disappointed with the situation.

She finally gathered the courage to look at me. I could see regret in her puffy eyes, "I'm sorry. I got caught up in the Interweb thing."

"Look," I took a deep breath and said, "I know you had good intentions, but deceiving me by sending me your daughter's picture instead of yours is not the right thing to do." She shook her head in agreement and said she would never do it again.

After paying the check I walked her to her car. It was getting late and I didn't want to be here after dark. I'd enough trouble with these country roads during the day. As I turned to leave she felt compelled to say, "You're a nice guy. Would you like to meet my daughter?"

"Nah," I said, imagining what that possible meeting would be like, "I'll take my chances on the Interweb."

Chapter 4: Some Like It Hot

I'd like to begin this chapter by having you perform an Internet search of the names Valeria Lukyanova and Lolita Richi. Go ahead, I'll wait.

By now you know both these ladies claim to be human Barbie dolls. What would compel these women to make such drastic changes to their appearances just to impress others? In their words, they wanted to "look perfect." This might seem rather extreme, but some people insist on changing their outward appearance to suit the idealized images of society.

It was a dreary fall evening in 1998: overcast, rainy, chilly but not cold. On days like these I spent most of my free time after work online. That was my first mistake. Focusing on the possibility of meeting someone without the proper amount of sunlight and food can lead to bad mistakes, and quite possibly, vampirism.

While surfing online I happened to come across a profile that spoke directly to me. I was impressed by her direct but flirtatious words, and once I saw her picture I was stunned. Too good to be true, I thought. Her beauty was breathtaking. She had a face like a porcelain doll, big expressive eyes, and dark red lips that would be heaven to kiss. Her body was slender and curvy, and she was leaning provocatively against an ornate wooden door. The cracked wood grain on the weathered door was a stark contrast to her golden hair and flawless skin.

I fired off an email complimenting the woodwork on her front door, and asking about her interests and hobbies. Every guy would compliment her looks, so I made *sure* my approach was far from the standard one. Even though I thought she was incredibly attractive, I wanted to know what things we had in common. What good is a pretty face if all she does is sit quietly and never speak, or even worse, talk incessantly and never quit? If the conversation doesn't flow smoothly the first couple of dates, then it's best to move on. Ha! I've already started to fantasize about dating her even before her response!

Her email floated into my inbox on Friday. "Veronica" wrote about her dislike of having to date online, but felt this type of dating was better because she could be more selective.

"I've only been online for a day and have hundreds of emails. This is crazy!" she wrote.

We exchanged emails back and forth and I found we enjoyed common interests in windsurfing, movies, and traveling. When emailing became too cumbersome we switched to Internet Messaging (IM). Volleys of IM's kept me up late that night, and I felt we were beginning to share a deep connection.

I asked for her phone number. There was a long pause. Then she sent a picture of her dog "Buster". What?!? We chatted for a little longer and I asked her again. At this point I was worried she didn't feel the same as I did about a possible match.

"I'll give you my number if you promise not to call until later tomorrow," she typed.

It was close to 2 a.m. I was wired with excitement.

"Of course. I promise. I'll wait." I wrote in return.

"Here it is… Goodnight sweetie!" She gave me her number and I felt like I was one step closer to the holy grail.

"Good morning sugar!" I flirted back with her, "Do I have to wait 22 hours to call you, since technically, that would be tomorrow?"

"Call me when the sun is shining, silly boy. ;)~ "

I went to bed with her picture on my mind, the thought of her living alone with "Buster" and the imaginary sound of her soft, feminine voice.

My lucid dream of Veronica and Buster was crushed at 4:48 a.m. on Sunday morning when my phone rang. It was the security company I used for my business. A side door sensor had tripped at the main building and the alarm was blaring.

By the time I dressed, drove to the office, fixed a faulty alarm, and a calmed down a perturbed policeman, I arrived back home after 7 a.m. I felt more tired than when I left. The sun was cresting over the trees and I kept thinking about Veronica's last message. Now? Um, no. I flopped into bed and tried to tune into the previously televised dream.

When I finally did get up, I awoke startled, thinking I'd slept through Sunday. What time was it? 3:03 p.m. in the afternoon! Oh no! I fumbled through the papers next to my computer, found the used scrap of paper with her name scribbled on it, and a heart enveloping her phone number. As I dialed each digit, my heart was racing faster. This, in addition to the shock of waking up really, really late on a perfectly good Sunday afternoon, wasn't good for my state of mind.

After a few rings, a high-pitched, breathy, garbled voice entered my ear. "H-hello?"

"Is this Veronica?" I said in reply.

"Yes...is this Chris?" her voice was faint and hard to make out. I pressed my ear into the phone.

"It is...are you, okay?" Strangely I was mimicking her, although I was concerned that something was wrong.

"I've lost my voice...hard to talk," her words were scratchy and seemed far away.

We tried to continue the conversation, but her laryngitis and spotty telephone connection made communicating impossible.

"Maybe I should call when you get better. I would love to talk to you more and get to know you." I said, dreaming about the prospect of meeting this angel, regardless of how she sounded on the phone.

Throughout the week we sent IM and email messages to each other, and on a few occasions I called at random in the hope we could exchange the spoken word. Each time I called, a standard computer voicemail answered. She was considerate and always followed up with an email message explaining her voice wasn't getting any better.

Although I only knew her for a little more than a week, by Friday morning I was determined to meet her face-to-face. She lived close to Miami and I felt it would be great to get together, but knew a relationship would probably never work because of the distance. My hope was that maybe, just maybe, we would hit it off and she would move to Savannah. I decided to take a plane trip from Savannah to Miami. You might think this was crazy. Heck, I would have to agree with you. I later found out I was suffering from "Internet infatuation." This is the feeling of a complete connection to someone you met on the Internet after baring your soul to them. I was excited and couldn't wait to see her. Also, a trip to Miami was a chance to leave town.

"This will be a lot of fun!" I kept telling myself.

"If I don't go now, she might meet another guy and I'll never get to see her." my mind was racing with the possibilities of losing out to an imaginary adversary.

I searched for airline tickets to Miami, and found a 6 a.m. Saturday morning flight leaving out of Savannah. I planned to return at 6 p.m. Sunday. With such short notice and the skyrocketing price of fuel, the ticket cost was astronomical. At the "discounted" rate of $456, it was also non-refundable.

Seconds after I confirmed my flight, her IM popped up on my screen.

"How is my handsome man?" she typed as her avatar in the message box changed back and forth to compliment her mood.

"I'm doing excellent. How are you today? What are you doing tomorrow?" I asked coyly, not letting on to my intentions.

"Oh nothing," she typed "I was planning to see a movie or have lunch with some friends. What are your plans?"

"I am going on an adventure," and left my conversation at that.

"Really? I haven't been on any adventures in a long time." she typed, adding a smiley face for good measure.

I thought it might be a little creepy to tell her I bought an airplane ticket and was planning to be in Miami the next morning. Looking back I can see this was one of those "what the hell was I thinking?" moments.

We chatted for a couple of hours, then I realized that I would need to get to bed soon to make my 6 a.m. flight.

"I have to go. I need to get up early tomorrow to take a trip," I typed.

"Where are you going? I really want to know!" She pressed me for more information.

"I'm heading South. I might be able to see you tomorrow if you have the time." I sat back and waited for a response.

"OMG! REALLY? OMG! OMG! OMG! OMG! OMG! OMG!" At that moment the IM window froze. My guess is it was from the sheer amount of excitement we were both feeling at that moment. I shutdown my computer and went to bed.

My alarm chimed at 4:17 a.m. and I sprung from bed. I hate having an early flight. My mind is on high alert all night and I usually can't sleep. When the alarm finally rang, it was like zapping my tongue with a fresh 9 volt battery.

I packed for this impromptu trip the day before, so it was easy to get ready. I dressed and quickly made it out the door. My airline-approved overhead luggage bag was packed like I was expecting to visit for a week. I was a little nervous, wanting to make a good first impression.

All early morning travelers are anxious but slow moving, standing in line to get their tickets. Before electronic tickets, travelers booked their flight and picked up their boarding passes at the ticket counter. My phone rang as I was standing in line with a lethargic group of Latino and overly tanned people returning to Miami. I didn't recognize the number and let it ring, thinking that whoever it was had drunk dialed me at 5:05 a.m. on Saturday morning. I got my boarding pass, made my way through security, and was walking to the gate when my phone rang again. I glanced at the number and realized the area code was from Miami! I frantically swung open my new flip phone, and pressed it to my ear expecting to finally hear Veronica's clear, crisp voice.

It was a female voice, but not one I knew, "NO, YOU CAN'T COME! You don't understand who this person really is!" She told me "Veronica" was actually a transvestite who'd paid to have his pictures altered to look more feminine.

"What!?!" My scream could be heard echoing throughout the somber terminal. Then the anonymous woman sent me an unretouched photo of the dude. Ay Caramba! That was my first introduction to a program called Photoshop. I slumped into a nearby chair and compared the photo she sent me to the profile picture I printed out. His Adam's apple was bigger than mine, but with a couple of keystrokes in Photoshop it was gone. I could now see hairy arms, a masculine jaw, and other facial and body features that must have taken 50 graphic designers a couple of months to correct. But there he stood, wearing the same dress as the one in the picture I'd seen on Veronica's profile just a week earlier. I was on the verge of vomiting. As the color left my face, the attendant at the gate asked if I needed assistance. I didn't totally pass out, but I do remember sliding off the chair and laying on top of my overnight bag. I felt sick at the thought of actually meeting her, I mean him, I mean whoever that was. The most horrible part was putting my trust in someone who had fooled me. My infatuation had been so strong I'd dropped $456 on a non-refundable plane ticket.

I don't remember how long I stayed hunched over my bag, staring at the printed photo of my fantasy girl. My world closed in around me as I focused blankly ahead. The ringing in my head began to drown out the sound of the airport, and it seemed like I was stuck in an infinite loop of disbelief, sadness, and disgust.

"Sir" a muffled voice began to penetrate my protective shell.

"SIR!" the voice finally caught my attention.

I slowly cocked my head to the side to see the bowed legs of a pot-bellied security guard, and behind him, a male and female paramedic. The guard tilted his head to meet my dumbfounded gaze.

"Is everything okay?" He looked back over his shoulder and whispered to the paramedics, "Do you think he's had a stroke?"

After realizing I was only dazed, the paramedics flanked me on both sides and helped me to a nearby chair. Passengers were boarding as all this was happening, but I wasn't in any hurry to get on the plane.

"We will be departing in five minutes," the counter attendant mentioned to the crew standing around me, "we'll have to leave him behind."

"That's okay," I said, causing everyone to whip their heads in my direction. "I don't think I'll be going to Miami anytime soon."

"Do you remember what you were doing before you passed out?" The male paramedic asked as the female paramedic checked my blood pressure and measured the degree of dilation of my pupils. When my eyes were able to focus again, I realized there WAS a female paramedic and began to blush. This was awkward.

"Wow, she's a beauty!" the guard remarked as he looked at Veronica's printed picture. "Was she the reason why you were making the trip? Damn, I'd like to meet her!"

I thought to myself, "If you only knew."

The male paramedic took a closer look at the picture and then back at me. "You know, this picture looks altered. It's a very good likeness of someone. I have a cousin who's a photographer and he makes computer changes to pictures all the time. Are you a graphic artist?"

I shook my head no, closed my flip phone, and put it in my pocket before anyone else saw the "real" Veronica. In the 20 minutes it took me to return to normal, the male paramedic was quick to point out common mistakes of computer editing:

missing shadows, mismatched skin colors, body parts out of proportion.

"By the way, where does your cousin work?" I prodded the paramedic.

"He's...he's in Miami." he said as he glanced at me from the corner of his eye.

"Small world," I said.

"Yes, very, very small world," the paramedic smiled.

Chapter 5: Valley of the Dolls

I don't ever want to grow up. Sometimes I wish I could play games all day, eat candy, stay up late, and live as if everyday was summer vacation. Problem is, when we take those childhood habits into adult life, society labels us as quirky and makes us feel like outcasts since we don't "act our age."

We all hold on to some remnant of our past. Maybe you have a comic book or two, or models of airplanes and cars, or clothes from an era that matches your music collection. It's tangible evidence we lived through that time, good or bad, and brought a souvenir with us. These artifacts hold an emotional bond to a time we yearn to return to and feel safe again. But we all know we can't go back home again. Or, can we?

I met Linda on OkCupid. She had a look of childish wonder, and a mischievous grin in several of her pictures. Her profile was humorous, describing her lust for chocolate as requiring several years of rehab after violating a restraining order to never set foot again in Hershey, Pennsylvania. Her heart-shaped face and high cheekbones made her eyes more prominent. Maybe it was the angle of the camera, but her eyes were the center of attention in every one of her pictures. Her straight dark hair was draped over the front of her shoulders, neatly parted on the side, and framed her face beautifully. One of her favorite hobbies was running, and I could tell by her fit body and chiseled calf muscles that her hobby was more of a career.

There was a quality about Linda that drew me to her, a playfulness I really wanted in a relationship. The dates I had been on recently were more like interrogations, with both sides asking questions to solve some weird relationship crime. I wondered what it would be like to return to the kindergarten way of finding a girlfriend. If I could only walk up to a woman, hand her a note that said, "I like you. Do you like me? Check one of the boxes below." Being the trickster that I am, there would only be two "yes" boxes. Either she would laugh and we could begin the relationship or she would hand the message back to me and say "Um, no thanks."

Nothing is ever that simple.

I sent Linda an email and we quickly proceeded to talking on the phone before we met. She liked the personal interaction of phone conversations instead of email and felt comfortable enough to meet for lunch. We decided to meet at a local coffee shop that serves an organic selection of sandwiches, salads, and entrees.

"Meet me there at 11 a.m. this Sunday," I said.

"Sounds great! See you then!" she sounded excited and energetic, just like her profile.

On Sunday morning I entered the coffee shop with five minutes to spare and looked around for Linda. The place was relatively quiet and reserved, an indication she probably wasn't here yet. I sat and waited to see when she would walk through the door.

Looking over the menu on the wall I decided on the breakfast burrito, but didn't order since my date hopefully was enroute.

Ten minutes later, no sign of Linda. I checked my phone and sent her a text. She texted back saying she was running a little late but would be there soon.

Twenty minutes later Linda came walking through the door. Dressed in a multi-colored tie-dyed t-shirt tied in a knot at her waist, dark purple cut off jeans and a pair of red and black bowling shoes with white frilly socks. It was hard to believe this woman was in her 30's.

"Hellllooo Chris!" she greeted me with open arms and a big kiss on the cheek.

"Why helllooo Linda!" I replied. We locked arms and strode to the front counter.

Linda ordered five cookies, a banana-strawberry smoothie, and a hard-boiled egg. My previous decision to order the breakfast burrito was unchanged.

The cashier gave us a trophy as a marker so the waiter would know where we were sitting. The trophy was of a soccer player with a big number one perched high on a plastic pedestal.

Linda grabbed the trophy out of my hand and started waving it high over her head yelling, "We're NUMBER ONE! We're NUMBER ONE! Whoo-hoooo!" and laughed.

The cashier rolled her eyes like she's heard this many times before.

We picked out a table against the far wall to get a good view of the eclectic mix of people who inhabit Savannah. SCAD students entered the shop with brightly colored hair and piercings in every orifice. Sweaty tennis players and runners that circle Forsyth Park came in for a break from the oppressive summer heat. Hipster moms and dads wheeled their hipster babies dressed in clothing from both Goodwill and Urban Outfitters.

When our food arrived, Linda devoured her five cookies, "I always eat dessert first. Because life's too short and I LOVE cookies!" she said with a mischievous grin.

"You're dressed very colorfully today," I remarked at her clothing choices.

"I LOVE colors and rainbows and I'm a child of the light! There is an aura around you too! I see a bright blue aura around your head. That means you have a very calm personality and are open to new possibilities." She waved her hands in circles around my face to indicate where my aura was located.

"Really? You can see my aura?" I was a bit skeptical but intrigued.

"Of course I can! Everyone has an aura and you can see them too if you have an open mind and heart. See that woman over there? Her aura is white!" She pointed to a mother with her new baby.

I squinted to see if there was a halo of white light around the woman she identified. "I don't see it. Is the aura close to her body?"

"Not too far away from her body, but close. White means purity of spirit. She must be so in love with her baby!" Again she waved her hands to indicate the position of the light, since I was clearly in the dark. The lady in question looked up from her baby and Linda waved and smiled to cover up the fact that she was reading her aura without permission.

When Linda turned back to look at me, I noticed she was wearing a crystal pendant.

"Your necklace is very unique. Is that quartz?"

"Yes! It helps me to absorb energy. This is an energy crystal. It was given to me by a shaman at last year's Bumbershoot," she beamed with glee.

"Wait, what's a Bumbershoot?" I said, not understanding what form of English she was speaking.

"Bumbershoot is a music festival where people can be free and dance and play. I met a shaman who held the power to stop time and he gave me this crystal. It has magical powers and can summon unicorns and fairies!" She laughed and swung the crystal like a pendulum between her fingers.

"You believe in unicorns and fairies? Honestly, I can't say that I do." I looked at her and frowned.

"Well, that's my form of religion. I'd rather believe in something magical than nothing at all," she leaned in to whisper, "have you ever lost a sock?"

"Is there a unicorn out there wearing my odd socks?" I said, stunned. "I've always wondered why I can't keep a pair longer than a few weeks." This could explain the origin of static cling, I thought, imagining mythical creatures using my dryer like a hamster's treadmill.

"No, it's the FAIRIES that take socks. That's how they play with humans. Now you know fairies exist!" She was happy to show me I could now believe in something.

"How does the crystal work? Do you wave it over your socks before you put them in the wash? Does it work for all socks or is there a special crystal for athletic socks?" I asked, then noticed she wasn't paying attention to me, but playing peek-a-boo with a child at a nearby table. After we talked for a bit longer, we decided to go to a movie. She wanted to see the latest installment of Toy Story. The local theater was always so cold, in my estimation, it doubled as a meat locker. Being the middle of summer, we weren't properly dressed for a frozen matinee.

"Oh, I live a few blocks away. Let's stop by my place so I can get my sweater and change out of these uncomfortable shoes." she said rubbing the sore arch of her right foot. As we left the restaurant, she grabbed the bread from a half-eaten sandwich discarded by a previous customer. "It's for the ducks," she said wrapping the bread pieces in a napkin and stuffed it in her purse.

I drove her home and she invited me up to her apartment. I was in awe when I stepped inside her living room. Shelves lined every wall. On each shelf were dolls of every conceivable size, shape, and color. Not just a few dolls, but enough to make the people of Belpre (the Doll Capital of the World) jealous. Each wall overflowed with porcelain faces and plastic eyes staring at me from every direction. The room was silent. With the exception of a few lit candles, the only light streaming into the room came from a lone window draped in colorful scarves.

Linda emerged from her bedroom with a jacket and a small satchel. "Have you ever had a Tarot card reading?" She asked me with raised eyebrows.

"No, I can't say that I have. I've always wanted one though."

"Great! You sit over here and I'll lay out the cards. You shuffle and cut them first." She motioned to a small table and two chairs in the corner.

After I fumbled with the oversized cards and dropped half of them on the floor, at her direction I shuffled and cut them twice and put the tarot cards in a pile on the table.

"Now, put your hand on the cards," she said. As I did, she placed her hands on top of mine and started chanting an incantation. I couldn't make out what she was saying, but I thought it sounded like the song Peanut Butter Jelly Time.

After the incantation she waved her hands over the cards and declared them "ready."

"Now, you need to ask the cards a question. It can be anything you want to know." This was the first time I sensed she was serious.

I closed my eyes and came up with a question. When I opened my eyes I shook my head yes to confirm. She picked up the cards and placed two cards in a cross, one on top of the other, then four cards at each point of the cross, then four cards in a line beside the cross.

"The first card tells us the heart of the matter," she flipped the card over showing a man in robes holding a wand high in the air in his right hand. Above his head was the symbol for infinity. It was the Magician. Linda sat back in her chair, took a deep breath, then closed her eyes to think of an answer.

WHAM! Without warning there was a flash of light and the table flipped over. Tarot cards went everywhere. We both jumped from our chairs and screamed in surprise.

"What the hell was that?" I was still shaking from the adrenaline rush.

"I...I don't know! That's the first time I conjured a ghost at a Tarot card reading!" Linda was overjoyed.

"A what? I don't think it was a ghost," I tried to compose myself as I helped her pick up the Tarot cards.

"Well, there's only one way to find out if it was a ghost! You must draw a card from the Tarot deck three separate times. If you get the same card, it was definitely a ghost," Linda said confidently.

"What will that prove?" I said, thinking that the probability for such an occurrence was extremely rare. I turned the table and chairs upright and we sat back down.

"Are you afraid I might be right?" She challenged me, handing me the deck.

"No, this is silly. I'll do it to put your mind at ease," I took the cards from her hand and started shuffling them. Placing them on the table, I cut them into two separate piles, then placed one pile on top of the other. "Okay, let's get this over with so we can see the movie."

I took the top card off the deck and turned it over. It was the Magician. Linda's eyes got wide. "Beginner's luck," I said. No such things as ghosts. "Here, you shuffle them."

Linda picked up the cards and started shuffling them. She placed them in front of me and I cut the cards three times, placing different stacks on top of each other.

I took the top card off the deck and turned it over. It was the Magician. My eyes got wide and Linda stood up from her chair.

I looked through the deck to see that they were all different. They were. Very strange indeed.

I took my time to shuffle the Tarot deck, then handed them to Linda to shuffle them again. She placed them on the table before me and I cut the cards in four separate piles. I had her put one pile on top of another, then I put one pile on top, and she finished by topping the deck with the last pile of cards.

In a standard Tarot deck, there are 78 cards, each of them different. The probability of selecting the same card three separate times after two people independently shuffled and cut the cards is 1 in 474,552. If the Magician showed up a fourth time, the odds would be 1 in over 37 million! I looked at the top card and took it off the deck. When I turned it over Linda screamed. It was the Magician, again!

Moments earlier, high above our heads and camouflaged by the sea of dolls, was a white cat waiting to pounce. At just the right moment he struck, jumping on the edge of the table, causing it to flip and frightening us both. He quickly scurried under the darkness of a nearby chair, undetected. After Linda's scream at the Magician's draw, he shot out from under the chair and ran up and down the shelves knocking off doll after doll in his wake. Porcelain doll heads shattered as they hit the hardwood floor, making it sound like a succession of gunfire. Shelves collapsed and toppled on each other as the cat made his way to the bedroom door and safely hid under Linda's bed.

"See! There WAS a ghost here! It scared Pumpkin out of this room and under my bed! Cats are very aware of psychic disturbances and now this proves it!" Linda exclaimed as she walked to the kitchen.

"Really? It was just coincidence. I think your scream scared the cat." I was able to piece together the cat toppling the table, but was still unsure about the spooky four card draw.

"You must go, I have to smudge the apartment. I don't want my Pumpkin to be afraid," Linda rushed to the kitchen and brought back a smoldering collection of what looked like twigs wrapped in twine.

"What is that? It smells horrible!" I stood up to move out of Linda's way. She took the twigs and shook them in the corners of the room, then at the table, then at each of the dolls left on the shelves.

"Okay then, I can see this will take a while," I said, walking to the door.

"Um, hmmm," Linda knew I was leaving, but was engulfed in her own little world of conjured ghosts, shattered dolls, and putrid smoke.

Considering the amount of time she was spending with each

doll, she's probably still there smudging her apartment.

Chapter 6: White Fang

Perfection is impossible, especially in relationships. No one is going to fulfill your every desire, and I assure you someday you will disappoint your partner. That's life. You learn to make compromises. It's important to realize the other person is not going to change their annoying habits or throw away that dingey 1970's Led Zeppelin t-shirt. Differences and imperfections make us unique and gives us something to talk about.

Enter Lady Gwendolyn stage right. To say she was very prim and proper was an understatement. In her words, she "had no luck finding someone online that met her high standards." Granted, she was as uptight and stiff as a person could be. All her movements were slow and graceful. She constantly checked her seams and the position of every hair on her perfectly coiffed head. Cleanliness was her superpower, and the two maids who cleaned her home could probably attest there was no one as strict about ridding the world of dust and dirt.

I originally saw her profile on Plenty of Fish, a singles website growing in popularity.

My instincts were telling me that this woman was probably not for me. She was very pretty but looks can be deceiving. There are many traits (or unforeseen problems) that make shining profiles tarnished in real life. Everything in her profile screamed "FLAWLESS". (Take note, when everything in a picture is perfect, there's always something just outside of the frame waiting to mess things up.) In fact, she used words like "unblemished", "pristine", and "impeccable" several times in her profile. Her pictures were taken by a professional photographer. Nothing was out of place. Her hair was set in stone. Every fiber of her clothes aligned neatly in sharp, straight, crisp lines. I asked in my initial email if she was a model for a catalog.

"No, why would you ask that?" she replied.

"Because your pictures are so...professional. Most people just put candid photos of themselves on this site. I've never seen such attention to detail." I responded.

"I'm not perfect, but I'm very, very close," her ego chimed in.

"Would you have time for conversation over coffee or tea?" I wanted to see how close she really was to perfection.

"I have this weekend free if you'd like to meet," she said.

We worked out the logistics. Her day consisted of work, exercise, and something she called her "daily cleanse." She also needed to attend to her "babies". I checked her profile twice and it confirmed she didn't have kids or pets.

The spot she chose for our meeting was trendy and very expensive. This restaurant served food tapas style. If you haven't heard of this type of dining, tapas is Spanish for "expensive child's plate." I was subjected to eating bits of food off tiny plates that cost a small fortune. This unique opportunity to eat a meal that would easily fit into a teacup set me back $84.

Was I missing something? Did the chef start off with a 16 ounce Porterhouse steak, zap it with a shrink-ray, and serve it up on a Triscuit? The look of surprise on my face was more incredulous with each of the four samples brought to our table. Most courses were a bite at most, and with someone else sharing the dish, I felt as if I was doling out rations on a lifeboat adrift at sea.

"Mmmmmm...chef Arnold is my favorite!" she exclaimed as she cut her teeny portion into an even smaller molecule of food.

She must have arrived early for the secret psychedelic 'shroom salad.

My date was the type of woman you would see at the opera in a full length dress. But she would dress this way even if there wasn't an opera for a thousand miles. A speck of dirt would never touch her body. She would never let her hair down, slouch, or spit. I imagined any fun in her life would require major pre-planning, and forms filled out in triplicate.

Meeting her at the restaurant confirmed she was as straight-laced and impeccable as her photos. Our conversation veered to relationships, and I asked her what she was looking for in her "ideal" man.

"There is no such thing." she said, "My father was the only ideal man. And then of course, there's Jesus."

I looked at her from the corner of my eye, "Really? It must be difficult for you to hold such high standards for your potential boyfriend. I don't know your father, and I'll never be as good as Jesus. Heck, Jesus had 12 best buddies and thousands of followers. I have a hard enough time keeping up with my friends on Facebook."

She laughed. This was the most surprising event of the date so far. Then she smiled. Another amazing thing! I was getting worried that she wasn't human. Then she leaned forward and put her hand on her face. Oh, no! A hair had mistakenly wiggled out of the tight bun cemented to her head and was lying on her cheek. A shriek of terror echoed through the restaurant and caused everyone (well, the couple sitting five tables over) to look and wonder.

"I will be right back," she said as she dashed to the nearest restroom. Fortunately for her, it was the woman's restroom.

Twenty two minutes later she returned. "I almost thought you had left out the back door," I quipped jokingly and pointed at her cheek. "I see you wrangled the stray."

"I don't like messes. You should have not seen me that way. I apologize. It's just...just that I want everything in my life to be exactly how I want it to be."

"You know that isn't realistic. Life has a way of making things imperfect. Chaos creeps in. Entropy takes over. Life is a mess, just don't make it a mess for someone else."

I think what I said struck a nerve. Her face softened. For a brief instance she looked relaxed and at peace.

Through the restaurant glass window we heard the muffled sounds of someone talking loudly. The entrance door swung open and a stocky woman dressed in a black leather biker jacket, blue jeans and boots came stomping in, yelling into her cell phone.

"You goddamn liar!," she shrieked.

I saw Gwen look at the woman and they exchanged visual contempt for each other. I could tell there was friction between them both, but didn't know the back story.

The biker woman strode to the bar, ordered a beer, and continue to rant at the person on her cellphone before slamming it on the bar.

"That's my younger sister, Joyce," Gwen said in disgust.

Joyce heard her and swiveled around on her bar stool to meet her gaze.

"Love you too, sis." Joyce raised her beer and took a big swig.

"I hear you and Jake split up." Gwen said, "What's going to happen to Corey?" Gwen seemed to be throwing spears at this point, trying to get Joyce to either leave or start a catfight.

"Say, why don't you take your gossip and go! My life isn't any concern of yours. And Corey and I will do just fine, with or without Jake." Joyce spat.

"You'll mess up your son's life just like your own. I always wanted you to finish school, and explore life before starting a family. But you had to be a rebel and get pregnant at 19! Now you have to live with your life choices." Gwen was turning red at the thought.

"Indeed I do. I don't care what you think of me and what plans you had of my future. I am doing what I think is best for my kid so leave me the hell alone." Joyce tilted her head back and guzzled the remaining bottle of beer. She threw a few dollars on the bar to cover her tab and stormed out the door.

After Gwen simmered down and Joyce was out of sight, I asked Gwen if she would be interested in seeing the latest art exhibit at a nearby gallery.

"I have finer art at my home. We should go there instead." At that moment I'd thought we made a connection. She looked at me and motioned for me to move closer. As I leaned in, she slowly reached up to my face, readjusted my collar, and gave me a nod of approval.

As we were leaving I noticed that Gwen had a take-home box.

"I thought we finished all four tapas plates. What was left over?" I said, astonished.

"Oh, I usually get the after dinner mints to go since I'm so stuffed."

Gwen and I got in our separate cars and I followed her home. Well, it wasn't exactly a home, more like a castle. On what looked like a hundred acres, sitting on a hill, was a large, expansive palace. A finely trimmed lawn and hedges led up to a dual marble staircase with 12 foot high oak entrance doors. The walls were all white brick with white turrets and white slate shingles.

When I parked in the driveway, she got out of her car and told me to park near a small area covered by trees. She didn't want her neighbors to see my car (with a telescope, I assume), possibly because there was dirt from the road on the bumper. She also told me to use the entrance in the garage, after removing my shoes and using the special foot bath.

"What is this place?" I thought to myself. "Is it some sort of clean room where she makes semiconductors or experiments with viruses?"

I walked into the garage with my shoes in hand and was greeted by Maria, one of Gwen's two maids. Maria was in her 40's, stout in stature, with an olive complexion and puffy eyes. She was wearing a modern maid's uniform that was pressed and impeccably clean.

"Chris?" She looked at me intently and walked around me as though I was contagious. "Before you go inside I need to explain a few things to you."

The look on my face probably mirrored my internal thought of "What now?" Maria walked me through the rules of the house, and asked me to repeat each rule as she told it to me. She kept saying, "Be mindful of her 'babies'". All the while I wondered if I needed to update my life insurance policy.

Then came the big reveal. When I entered her house, I was in awe. The main room was huge, with 20 foot ceilings, and EVERYTHING in white. White carpet, white furniture, white walls, white tables, white, white, white. Scratch that. Not everything was white. Her "babies" were actually very rare and expensive orchids from around the world placed in each room of her home. With everything around them a brilliant white, it was extremely easy to see the vibrant colors and delicate forms of these flowers.

Gwen emerged from a side room in a white kimono and silk slippers. She showed me almost every room of her house and went into elaborate detail about the history and description of the orchid in each room.

At the end of the tour we sat on a formal, white settee in a small room next to a hallway. The settee had no back and was placed in the middle of the room. Flanked on each side of the settee were two of her largest orchids in ornate hand-painted white pots. Gwen sat upright, poised and proper as ever. We were closer than before, and I sensed she was finally comfortable with me. I leaned in and kissed her, delicately but with purpose. She showed a very hard exterior to the world, but as I pressed my lips against hers I could feel her soften. I moved back away from her to see her expression, and she smiled broadly. Relieved to have made it this far, I relaxed and leaned back.

With nothing to stop me from reclining, I started to flip off the back of the settee. I reached for the armrest only to grab the lip of the large, ornate, hand-painted white pot. Oh. no.

As my body fell backwards, the pot rolled with me, rotating and throwing dirt everywhere. The orchid snapped in two and I could hear Gwen gasp and choke back a scream.

Dirt went flying into the white rug, white settee, white curtains, and white walls. I was covered in dirt as well, and one of the orchid flowers managed to wedge itself into the space between my ear and head.

Once the shock wore off Gwen's face, her expression turned to rage.

"Get out. Get out. GEEEET OUUUUUUT!" She yelled at me and pointed to the door several times. I stood up, brushed the dirt off my shirt, emptied out my pockets and pant cuffs back into the cracked flower pot, and quietly walked to the door.

As I left I was met again by Maria. She held my shoes and socks out in front of me in her outstretched arms. My shoes were clean, socks pressed. I thanked her and made my way out of the garage. The sun was fading over the horizon, but I could tell that my car had been washed and vacuumed. At least there were a few consolation prizes for today's date.

Sitting at the stoplight on my way out of town, who happened to pull up beside me on her motorcycle, but Joyce. At least I thought it might be her. She was wearing the same leather jacket I saw earlier, goggles, and no helmet.

"Hey! Nice bike!" I shouted over the rumbling idle of her motorcycle.

Joyce turned her head to look at me and realized who I was.

"Aren't you my sister's date? I thought you would be enjoying her company for the evening," she said, rolling her eyes. "What do you see in her?"

"Not much of anything, anymore. It was our first AND last date. I mistakenly toppled over one of her prized orchids. I'll never see the inside of that place again." I frowned.

"Ha, ha, ha! You should have seen that coming. I was surprised she let you inside her 'white castle'."

"Say, would you like to get a coffee and chat for awhile? You're much less uptight than your sister," I meant it as a joke, but I could tell Joyce was offended.

"Nah. I don't take my sisters hand-me-downs." She flicked her middle finger at me and took off on her motorcycle, squealing her back tire, leaving me with the smell of burnt rubber.

Oh well. Nothing beats getting rejected by two women on either end of the spectrum in one day.

Chapter 7: Crime and Punishment

The prospect of finding a 'soulmate' can seem daunting when you consider the number of people in this world. Out of the billions of people living on this planet, there has to be someone who meets all my criteria, has the same values, and doesn't mind that I eat animal crackers in bed. My friend Earl always used the expression, "Even a blind pig can sometimes find truffles." I had the same positive outlook, but eventually became more pessimistic the longer I tried dating online.

From the standpoint of online dating, it's possible to find the woman of your dreams. On one occasion I stumbled on a very alluring and sexy photo on OkCupid.com. I distinctly remember her piercing light blue eyes, demure and confident smile, and long locks of dark brown hair falling onto her tanned shoulders. What really interested me more was her online profile that mirrored my preferences, likes, and ideals almost identically. I just had to meet her!

"Hello Diane, I saw your profile and was interested in learning more about you. We have many of the same interests (all of them to be exact), and have similar ideas about online dating (did you copy my profile?). Just kidding. Write back when you have a chance and we can chat and hopefully meet soon."

My email to her was casual, but did convey my interest was genuine. We matched in every category, and our preferences for exact location, age, height, physical characteristics and hobbies were eerily identical.

Her response came seconds after I hit the "send" button, which didn't seem odd to me as this site tells members the identity of those viewing their profile.

"Hi Chris! I am very excited to know more about you and meet you in person! You look very handsome and yes, we are extremely compatible. I never thought I would get that lucky. I have over 16 pages of emails from this site, so if you don't mind I'd like your direct email when you reply. Diane."

We chatted more online, talked like old friends over the phone, then finally decided to meet for lunch at a local cafe.

When I arrived she was waiting at a table outside the cafe. It was a warm spring day, a welcome diversion from the damp winters and sweltering summers in Savannah.

She was dressed in high heel cork wedges, a short skirt that showed off her long, muscular legs, and a form fitting blouse that accentuated her ample breasts. On the side of her leg was a dragon tail twisting up and disappearing under the hem of her skirt. Although I was trying not to stare, she looked up and caught me admiring her ink.

The glint of silver bangles adorning her wrists sent off sparkles and partially blinded me. I squinted and made my way around the other tables to reach her.

She was sitting tall in her chair, sipping a sweet tea and adjusting her sunglasses. Her beauty caused time to slow down as I sensed the gravity of her feminine orbit and let me be pulled into her trajectory.

"You must be Chris!" she said and flashed a bright white smile. She turned to get out of her chair and stand up. I wasn't paying close attention to where I was as she moved forward. Within seconds we were two fingers shy of touching each other's noses.

Up close her skin looked flawless, and her perfume wafted into my nostrils and sent tingles down my spine.

"Ya-yes" was all I could muster. A little voice inside my head kept repeating "you'll wake up in five minutes and realize you didn't set your alarm, but this will be totally worth it."

Conversation flowed freely, and I was at ease almost immediately. It felt good to find someone genuinely interested in me who shared all of my desires and ideals. We talked about windsurfing and sushi, living on a tropical island, and travel to exotic locations. Between sharing dreams and banter she smiled, laughed, and touched my hand and knee. How did I earn a seat at the table with this incredibly beautiful and intelligent woman? I wholeheartedly wanted her to drop what she was doing, take the next flight out of town with me, and never look back.

Score one for online dating. A perfect match.

The topic of conversation turned to past cities we called "home". I gave a history lesson of places I lived, and my fondness for the people I met along the way. It was uncanny how she'd lived close to the areas where I'd resided, almost as if we'd taken the same life path just a few miles apart.

"And then I ended up in Savannah," I concluded, leaning back in my chair. I waited to hear how destiny brought her here.

Silence. The conversation train came to a dead stop. She pulled off her sunglasses and I could finally see into those light blue pools surrounding the pinpoints of her pupils. Her look turned quizzical as she furrowed her brow. "You never lived in Austin, Texas?" she said with great disappointment.

"No, I've never been there in my life." I offered with a weak smile. It pained me to say so.

"Damn, I thought you were the one." the glow of interest faded quickly from her face and she fumbled for her purse. I had the distinct impression this was some sort of test and for whatever reason I went from being an "A" student to flunking on a technicality.

"Is something wrong?" I asked, sensing her need to leave.

"Look, you're not the guy I'm contracted to find," she said shaking her head.

"Contracted? W-what are you talking about? Since when did the Mafia start hiring models?" I felt both relieved I didn't get "whacked" and mortified this was all a lie.

"I don't work for the Mafia," she smiled sweetly. "I'm a bounty hunter. See that guy over there?"

She waved to a shiny black 1988 Camaro parked with the engine running about a half block away. The guy behind the wheel looked rough. He was big and burly with a bushy mustache and curly black hair. His vintage dark sunglasses and Black Sabbath t-shirt probably came as a package with the car. He lifted a couple of fingers off the steering wheel to acknowledge her wave. Although I felt a strong connection to her, I hoped my evening didn't involve meeting any of her close friends.

"That's Rick. We get paid to bring in dead-beat dads. The guy we're looking for fits you almost exactly. Same age, born in your hometown, same height and weight, lives or recently lived in this area, does the same work that you do and has all the same hobbies."

Crap. I have a dead-beat doppleganger.

She leaned in, looking at me as if examining a diamond for obvious flaws, "Except, except you're too...nice. And you never lived in Austin."

Reaching to the chair beside her, she lifted her heavy black leather purse and dropped it on the table. The purse fell over and out popped a taser and a pair of handcuffs. Some people might think this was kind of kinky, until they saw the arrest warrant for the guy she was hunting. She was quick to stash all the "tools of the trade" back in her purse and signaled Rick she was ready to leave.

"It was good to meet you. Can't say that for the majority of guys I've met online. You're funny and will make some woman very happy someday," she assured me.

"Well, if I don't, then I guess I'll be seeing you again." She laughed out loud and smiled. I was glad I made the "best of the worst" list in her book.

She threw her purse over her shoulder and stood to go. As she did, I caught a glimpse of a college kid speeding up the sidewalk on a skateboard. The kid bumped her hard, and kept going only to look back and see her collide with the remaining drinks on the table. I saw what the hit-and-run skateboarder did not; the massive 300 pounds of muscle and dark hair blocking his path. The "wall of Rick" was impenetrable, especially to a scrawny 18 year old freshman late for art history class.

Rick grappled the kid by the shoulder with one hand, and the offending skateboard with the other. "Say you're sorry to the lady!" he growled. From the mean look in Rick's eyes, this wasn't the only punishment this kid might receive today.

"I-I'm s-s-sorry" the kid sputtered. "C-can I have m-my skateboard back?"

Rick sneered as he looked down at the kid, then saw the mess on Diane's clothes from the spilled drinks. In one fluid movement Rick held the ends of the skateboard and cracked it in half over his knee. I heard the kid whimper as his jaw dropped.

"There you go. Even trade for the mess you made." Rick handed the splintered skateboard halves to the devastated college kid and said, "Now, get the hell outta my face."

Diane tried her best to clean the stains from her blouse and skirt before she slid into Rick's Camaro. I watched as they made their way through tourist-crowded streets, turned down a side alley, and out of my life forever.

God help the man she was hoping to find.

Chapter 8: The Lady Vanishes

Eighty percent of success is showing up. You would think that I had plenty of success meeting women for offline dates because I showed up 100 percent. Nope! As it turns out, I was usually the lone man waiting for my date to show at the coffeeshop/restaurant/baseball game/bowling alley/shooting range.

Why the failure to launch? Beats me. I would confirm the date and time a few days prior and send a text or small chat again the day of the date. I would arrive at the location on time or early and wait. Time would pass and when I realized she didn't make it on time, I would either call or send a text. What usually happened if they weren't texting or calling me first? One of three things:

1. Crickets. No text reply. Radio silence. As if my date was pulling a Dick Cheney, transported to "an undisclosed location," and never heard from again.

2. The last second cancellation. If my date was sick or had an emergency, I gave them the benefit of the doubt and made contact a few days later to set up another date. If the woman was genuinely interested in meeting, we'd get together. If not, see number 1.

3. The late response. This was the most frustrating of the three. In this scenario, I wouldn't hear from her until the next day or later. Then she'd text/call/email me telling me she wanted to go out but either forgot, got lost, lost my contact information, lost track of time, met friends along the way, or some other lame excuse. I never replied to these women because no one is worth that much trouble.

I was stood up on dates more often than not, so I lowered my expectations of meeting anyone. I would usually bring a good book or plan on eating dinner at a restaurant by myself. Why waste time on someone who doesn't respect my time?

I know I'm not the only guy to have a "no show" date. However, with the advent of technology it's been much easier to flake out on meeting people.

In fact, the earliest recorded late date cancellation was between Claire Downing and John McGillicuddy, as documented in this Western Union telegram circa 1883:

JOHN, I TRUST YOU ARE WELL AND YOUR HORSE NO LONGER HAS THE COLIC STOP I HAVE BEEN WORKING ON THE FARM DAY AND NIGHT SINCE THE BOLL WEEVIL INFESTATION STOP MY APOLOGIES FOR NOT MEETING YOU YESTERDAY AT MISTER LARSON'S FEED STORE FOR A SARSAPARILLA STOP I ALSO LOOK DISHEVELED AS THE LOCAL BOYS HAVE TAKEN UP HAIRPIN PILFERING AND I CANNOT CONTAIN MY UNRULY LOCKS STOP MAYBE SOME OTHER TIME = CLAIRE DOWNING

Things haven't changed much since the 1800's, except that miscommunication is a hundred times faster.

I first contacted Stephanie through Zoosk. She was a retail manager at a clothing store in the mall. She seemed friendly enough in her profile, and we made plans to meet at a local coffee shop on Thursday after work.

I contacted her on Thursday morning to say hello and remind her that we were to meet at 6:30.

"That will be wonderful!" She texted back.

I went about my day and thought about her on occasion. Checking the local events, I noticed there was a band playing near the coffee shop tonight. If all went well, I intended to take Stephanie to see the band after meeting for coffee.

I left work a little early to prepare for the date and purchase tickets for the event. Luckily, I bought two tickets and decided if she didn't show I would pass her ticket on to someone else. Ten minutes before the date I was stuck in traffic and sent her a text letting her know I might be a little late. No response. Not good.

I made it to the coffee shop at 6:30 on the dot and saw she wasn't there. No text or missed call either. Hmmmm. I waited for fifteen minutes more, sent another text, and waited for a reply. Nada.

Instances like these make me think the worst has happened to my date. Did she get in an accident? Did her phone die and she couldn't contact me? Was she abducted by aliens and will require years of psychological therapy to adjust to the trauma? I never want to think that her lack of response is due to her indifference to me or dating in general. Or that she absent-mindedly forgot about our date. I flipped a mental coin and assigned things under her control to 'heads' and things outside her control to 'tails.' The coin landed on tails, so I decided tonight's no-show was due to solar flares that misdirected our text transmissions. I then ordered a hot tea and a turkey panini, had a leisurely dinner, and gave my extra ticket to a college student who could now enjoy the band for free. No harm, no foul.

At work the next day, I get a call from Stephanie.

"I'm soooo sorry I totally forgot about yesterday's date," she said.

"Did you get my texts? I was worried something happened to you. It seemed strange that you answered me in the morning, but I didn't get a reply later that day," I tried not to sound sarcastic.

"I don't know what happened. Honestly, I really want to meet," she said.

We made plans for another date, this time at the aquarium. She'd confided how she'd always wanted to go but couldn't find someone interested in accompanying her.

"See you tomorrow at 2 o'clock. I'll meet you in the lobby of the Marine Science Center," I confirmed.

"Yes, I'll see you then," she giggled and hung up.

I checked the weather for Saturday and noted that rainstorms were likely. Since we were meeting inside, a little rain wouldn't be a problem.

The next morning the sky was overcast. I sent Stephanie a text to plan ahead.

"Don't forget your umbrella, and our date...lol," I teased her.

"I have today off. I'll come prepared. Don't worry," she replied.

I did some errands and cleaned part of the house before I readied myself for today's potential date. The ominous sky kept darkening the closer our meeting time approached. Is this a bad omen? Lightning flashed outside and the roll of thunder came five seconds later. The rain was close as I watched the wind push tall pines from side to side. I left my home with ample time to be early for the date. Last time it was traffic due to an accident, this time it's Mother Nature. Neither are easily predicted and both create chaos on a daily basis.

I arrived at the Marine Science Center before the storm reached its peak. Only light rain fell on the roads, and I was happy to escape a heavy downpour. A few cars occupied the parking lot. A busload of young day-campers stood in a single file line outside the Center wearing identical dark blue rain ponchos. I parked on the end, away from the bus and near the edge of a retaining wall.

I went into the Center and was greeted by a teenager who had the unfortunate duty of working the weekend shift.

My date wasn't in the lobby (of course).

It started to pour bucket after bucket of a summer shower. All the day-campers quickly made their way into the entrance while holding hands. The last camper on the hand-holding train wasn't smiling as the hood had come off his poncho and water trickled down his clothes under the plastic protection.

"That was close," said the bus driver, a middle aged woman with a chubby face and small hazel eyes. Her hair was doused by the rain, but she managed to keep it up and away from her face while calming the children beside her.

Lightning struck just outside the building, temporarily blinding everyone who was turned toward the entrance door and window. The thunder crashed loudly, followed by the shrieks of several 11 year-old girl day-campers.

"That was closer," I said, hoping my date wasn't outside the door.

We were all thrust into darkness, and the only sounds now were the rain hitting the roof and side of the metal building, and children crying and moaning in fear. I had to get my bearings straight as I was one of the few adults here, and I could feel small hands clutching at my hands and legs for stability and comfort.

I turned on my cell phone and used the light to see who was around me. The bus driver did the same.

"It will be okay kids. Just stay still or sit where you are and get comfortable. We can wait this out," said the bus driver as she sat down on the floor. Ten or so children put their hands on me or sat near me, and the bus driver nodded in appreciation for the help.

Luckily, after 20 minutes the worst part of the storm passed by. The power was restored when backup generators restarted the filtration pumps to the aquariums and overhead lights.

"Yaaaaaaaaaaaay," the children screamed in relief. The bus driver gathered them all together to get them focused on looking at pretty fish for the next hour.

I looked at my watch. 2:25 p.m. No text or missed call, again.

"You missed the heaviest part of the storm, and kids screaming at lightning. All the fish survived. I'll wait if you're heading my way," I texted her and shook my head, my effort most likely futile.

At 2:45 there was still no reply, so I left the Center and headed out into the rain. There was no point in staying. Stephanie told me she would pay for the date since it was her blunder for not showing the first time. I flipped my mental coin and this time it came up heads, her fault.

The rain subsided and since I was close I took the opportunity to visit the mall. I also knew Stephanie had the day off, so she would be as far away from the mall as humanly possible. I also made sure not to enter the section of the mall where her store was located. What a pain to avoid awkward situations.

I finished shopping and headed home. It was late, so I stopped at a downtown restaurant to pick up dinner. Guess who I spotted there? Yes, you know who. I was standing at the order counter, looked over at the dining hall, and saw Stephanie eating with three of her friends. They were sitting at a booth near the hallway leading to the restrooms. I decided to go to the restroom while my food was being prepared, and lingered at a spot opposite Stephanie's table to hear all their gossip. There was a bulletin board in the hallway, I studied it intently, not raising any suspicions about why I stood there so long.

Eventually, the conversation on the other side of the wall turned to why Stephanie didn't have a boyfriend.

"I can't find the right guy for me, I guess. I want someone strong who loves to surf and has the body of an Adonis. He should be rich and travel the world. All I get on these loser dating sites are average guys with average lives," Stephanie whined.

When I got home there was a surprise waiting for me in my email inbox. Stephanie had written a nice note explaining that she really wanted to get together, but that her timing was off and just didn't feel a level of connection with me. Again, she apologized for not showing up at the aquarium (although she'd promised to take me out), and earlier for missing the coffee date. Guess what time THIS message was sent? Yep, 3:30 p.m. today. What a gal!

At this point I was fired up. All my creative juices were flowing and I just had to write. Of all the profiles I've written, I am proudest of this one:

Name: Andy "Riptide" Slade

Occupation: Semi-professional Surfer

Location: I travel extensively, so I may be visiting your town soon.

About me: I'm a laid back guy who was lucky enough to finish my business degree and inherit a large trust fund from my grandfather. Now I travel the world and surf, but am looking for the woman of my dreams to make my life complete. I don't want an average woman who wants an average life. You must understand business and be aggressive. A female manager for a retail store would understand my needs more than a girl who does nothing but party all the time. You must also love to travel and enjoy the finer things in life. If what I'm saying calls to you and you want the best, then write to me now.

I finished by specifying that Andy wanted women within 1-2 years of Stephanie's age, 5-10 pounds of her weight, 2-3 inches of her height, and ONLY her hair color.

I searched through Google pictures and came across a cool looking surfer dude with curly blonde hair and six-pack abs. He was leaning on a surfboard and had a bright white smile. Hello Andy!

The trap was set. All I had to do was wait.

Over the next week I received hundreds of emails. With my tightly focused profile, I had to respectfully decline any woman who didn't meet the highly specific criteria. I noticed that Stephanie looked at Andy's profile a couple of times the second day it was posted. She then returned to look at it 14 times on the fifth day. On the seventh day she viewed Andy's profile 21 times and finally sent an email:

"Hi Andy! Yes, your profile calls to me, and I can't believe how lucky I am to be reading it right now. I don't meet too many men who are savvy in business, love to surf, and travel the world. That's a unique combination. I work as a manager in a retail store and have a high appreciation for the finer things in life. When you get the chance and are in my area (are you visiting now?) we could get together for a glass of wine or dinner at a Conde Nast award winning restaurant. You can write to me on here, or my private email address, or call or text me when you like.

Love, Stephanie"

Bingo. I waited a couple of days before I replied to her message. I could see that she viewed Andy's profile incessantly over these two days, so I'm sure she was waiting for a reply from her dream guy.

"Aloha Stephanie! I'm on Maui now but will be in the Savannah area next week. Would you be able to get together on Thursday? I heard The Grey was a favorite of Conde Nast travelers, so let's meet there to kick things off. What do you say?

Andy"

I waited until 1 a.m. Eastern time to send the email and put 8 p.m. on the time stamp. This made it look like the email came from the Hawaii time zone. It took Stephanie less than 10 minutes to reply

"Oh yes! I'm available! Just tell me the time and I'll be there. Love, Stephanie"

I set up a reservation in Andy's name and emailed Stephanie to show up at 7 p.m. on Thursday. Then I waited until Friday morning to see what gold nuggets were in Andy's mailbox. Here they are:

"Andy, Where are you?"

"Andy, Are you okay?"

"Where the F**K are you???"

"You are such a F**KING A**HOLE for not showing up tonight. I don't believe how you can promise to meet with me, set up a date, and then not even call or text to tell me what's going on. That's so F**KING immature!"

Wow. It sounded like she was really pissed off in her email. Oh well, I waited until late afternoon to send her a proper reply:

"Stephanie,

I appreciate your time and efforts in trying to meet. Sometimes the stars don't align and even though we want to get together, we just can't. I think my timing may also be off with all the traveling I've been doing lately. When we first corresponded I was excited to get to know you, but now, I just don't feel a deep level of connection with you. Again, I apologize for not showing up at The Grey. Maybe I'll be back on my return trip from Japan. Sayonara, Andy."

She took down her profile the next day. Sometimes a dream stays just out of reach.

Chapter 9: A Rose By Any Other Name

Written communication can be misleading. As the amount of technology increases, face to face communication dwindles. Mix this with the myriad of acronyms used and numbers of emoticons popular in 'text speak', and it's no wonder confusion abounds.

Even with the ability to "Facetime," we still text more. We email and send Internet messages (IMs) that lack tone or inflection. There is no sarcasm in the subtext online, UNLESS YOU COUNT TYPING IN ALL CAPS AS SCREAMING AT YOUR READERS. You don't want anyone to think you're a maniac; not a prospective employer and certainly not a potential date. We all expect our intended audience to understand what we are writing about, only to find out later that we offended them or were misunderstood. If we could only turn back time and talk about the issues face-to-face instead of texting or sending an email, then many mistakes would be avoided.

It's rare for me to get an email first from a woman on a dating site, so I'm quick to respond if they take the initiative. I've sent out thousands of messages in hopes of connecting with the right person. But few women respond to my emails, and that gets discouraging.

Then one day I received this:

"Hi Honey! I see that you're adventurous and want to try new things. Me too! My friend is an engineer like you so I know you have a big brain. That's great, but I'm sure you have a creative and sensual side too. I haven't been on this site for a long time and am looking for someone like you who wants to enjoy more out of life!"

She seemed genuinely interested in me because she read my profile and took the time to write. I was pleasantly surprised to read her profile, and found her pictures to run the gamut from sweet and innocent to very sexy and alluring. It struck me as odd to receive an email from such a beautiful woman. I also learned she loved roses. A lot. In fact, the last line of her profile read, "Guys, you MUST bring roses to impress me."

I was glad to receive her reply so quickly. Considering the many likes and positive comments she received on her photos, I was intrigued to find out more about her and her life.

We corresponded back and forth, chatted over IM, then talked over the phone. She was funny, flirtatious, and had a very sexy voice. I was charmed and wanted to know more about her, but she remained mysterious and hoarded personal information, only letting it trickle out in droplets. She said I would find out more when we saw each other in person.

Early that morning I checked my inbox and was ecstatic to have received an email from her. "We should meet for a drink sometime," she said at the close of her message.

I waited until noon to call her, since she mentioned she worked late at night. I suggested we meet at an artsy coffee shop in downtown Savannah, but she insisted we get together at a bar on the other end of town. I agreed, excited at the thought of finally seeing her in person. After I hung up the phone she called back a few minutes later.

"Oh, if you really want a fun time, bring 120 roses with you." she giggled, said goodbye and hung up.

Wow! She REALLY loves roses! But that's going to be expensive, I thought. I'm sure I could talk to a florist and get a deal. Surely, she was joking. Wasn't she? I called back and waited as each ring made my heart race a little bit faster.

"Hi, I'm just calling to check I heard you correctly. That was 120 roses, right?" My palms were sweaty as I pressed the phone to my ear.

"You're right, honey. I look forward to seeing you." I could imagine her smiling on the other end of the line. At that moment

I was floating on a cloud, feeling a bit giddy at the thought of being close to her.

Then my left brain kicked in. As I hung up I calculated what it would cost to get that many roses. Thank god our meeting was months away from Valentine's Day or Mother's Day, or I would need a second mortgage on my house to buy her flowers on a regular basis. Hmmmm. Would she mind if I bought the roses from Sam's Club? I'm sure she could tell where I bought them if she is such a connoisseur. Would they have to be trophy winning roses? I search Wikipedia. There 100 species and 1000's of cultivars of roses. Holy Rose Parade, Batman!

I called my florist friend Tony to see if I could order direct from a grower, or if were are any other ways to get a huge amount of flowers by our date night.

After making several calls, Tony was able to find a grower with a large rose garden in the next state. He called me the next day to give me the good news.

"I need them in three days." I told Tony, "How much would that cost?" I waited, unconsciously holding my breath.

"Do they have to be all one color? I can get you a better deal if you don't want all red or pink," he told me over the phone.

He finally confirmed I could get 120 roses on the magic day. Fantastic! The roses wouldn't all be the same color, but I'm sure she will be impressed. In total, she would receive 10 bouquets of 12 roses. Sweet!

The day came when we were to meet. I left work early to reach the florist's shop before they closed. Tony greeted me at the door.

"We have your roses in the back. Did somebody pass away? Did you win the lottery? What the heck are you doing?" he looked at me as if I was crazy.

"I met someone who loves roses," I said with a cheesy grin on my face.

"Well, I have some bad new for you. I only have nine dozen roses. We were short a dozen because the other florist used them for a Get Well Soon basket." he peered out of the corner of his eye at me to see if this was going to be a problem.

My face turned red and voice raised an octave as I threw my hands up in the air at Tony. "Really?!? I drove from the other side of town just to pick up these roses and now you tell me that you don't have them all? This is terrible! You said you'd give me a great deal. You said you would have them by today. But, noooooooooooooooooooooooooooo! What the heck am I going to tell her? Oh, you're really great, but not worth 120 roses. Nope. Probably more like 108 roses. I don't think she'll be impressed." I sank down into a nearby chair, head in my hands.

"It's fine. Don't sweat it." Tony said as he put his hand on my shoulder. "I have some lovely irises, tulips, daisies, and...and hydrangeas! She would love hydrangeas! We have so many other flowers she won't notice if I mix them in a bouquet," he was throwing ideas at me, trying to prevent my meltdown from getting any worse.

"Okay, okay, that sounds good. Cover it up. But make it big. The bigger you can make it the better. I don't want this woman to think I'm a cheapskate," I looked at the back of the room and noticed eight bouquets of brilliant roses exploding in various colors. The mass of flowers covered the back wall, each batch looked like fireworks exploding from shiny silver vases. "Are those all...for me?"

"I hope you have a van," he said half jokingly. I felt my heart sink. My truck was in the repair shop, and I'd rented a compact car to make it back and forth to work.

I was resourceful and determined to take all of the vases with me. It took me 20 minutes to stuff the roses in my rental car. Four vases on the back floor, four vases in the back seat, and the huge vase of roses and other flowers in the front passenger seat. I was pricked by thorns and strained to push each bouquet in place without damaging the arrangements. Roses were sticking out of every automobile orifice. To my knowledge I don't think this was ever covered in the rental agreement.

Flowers were seat-belted in place and secured with boxes and towels. I slowed down miles ahead of any intersection. With my seat jammed fully forward, the air conditioner blasting cold air, and every square inch of the car covered in foliage, I was a mobile florist's display case on steroids. If I stayed too long at a stoplight I could hear an army of bees hot on my tail.

The sun was setting as I entered the parking lot of the Southside Bar. A few cars were in the lot, but I was lucky to get a spot close to the front door. After some difficulty I managed to get the heavy vase from the front seat. I struggled through the main entrance of the bar with my arms wrapped around the mass of flowers. I looked like a bouquet with legs. Everyone was staring at me, probably wondering why some guy was carrying a mountain of flowers into a bar.

Eddie the bartender looked up from the cocktail he was making. He was a tall, thin man with a square jaw and a very deep voice. Although the bar was primarily decorated in military memorabilia, Eddie was dressed in cowboy gear from head to toe. His roots were still very strong, as witnessed by his Longhorn hand gesture and "Hook em' Horns!" yell whenever the University of Texas came on TV.

"Who are those for?" Eddie questioned me, interested in knowing what was going on. "Did somebody die?"

"These are for my date. I was supposed to meet her here at 7 o'clock." I looked around and didn't see anybody who resembled her.

I heaved the flowers onto the bar, ordered a beer, and positioned myself to have a direct view of the front door. A few customers were sitting at a booth to the rear of the bar. A paunchy middle aged business man teetering on his stool looked at me and my flowers from the other side of the bar. His clothes were loosened, tie yanked to the side, as if he'd been tightly wound throughout the day, that at five o'clock his internal spring exploded.

"Those flowers are soooo beeaauuuuuuuuutifullllll," crooned the drunk businessman. He lifted his martini glass in a show of approval and smiled weakly. Then he gulped down what remained, waiving his empty glass in the air for a refill.

A few minutes later my date seductively sauntered into the bar. Her bright red dress hugged every curve and her neckline dove deep between her breasts. The fabric was silky with sheer side panels exposing her midriff and accentuating her hips. Her sexy high heels sparkled as they clicked on the linoleum floor. I was focused on her beautiful face and her bouncy blonde hair as she made her way to the bar. My heart was racing at the thought of kissing her soft, luscious lips.

She sat down on a barstool and ordered a fireball whiskey. She then looked my way, tilted her head and smiled. "You...you must be Chris."

I smiled back at her, and I moved over a few seats to sit next to her.

"Hey Eddie," she called to him from the bar, "Who died?" Pointing at the flowers and laughing.

"Nobody died. Those flowers are for you." He paused to see her expression. "Courtesy of your 'date'," Eddie turned his head to look at me, and then looked back at her and winked.

Her eyes widened and mouth popped open. "Wow, you're so...sweet." Her look of surprise and lack of enthusiasm made me wonder.

"I have the rest of your roses in the car," I said, smiling from ear to ear.

At this point the crocked businessman sitting at the end of the bar laughed so hard he fell off his stool and doubled over in pain. Everyone was now focused on the story unfolding between me and the lady in red.

"Oh...no. Really? I mean, that's great." She started to blush. Her voice was hesitant and slightly irritated. I knew something was wrong.

She leaned in closer and whispered in my ear "I hate to tell you this; I'm not the type of woman you're looking for. My interest isn't in roses, it's cash money."

Now it was my turn to blush. I couldn't believe what I was hearing.

The silence in the room was shattered by the loud ringtone of her cell phone. It was "Brick House" by The Commodores.

She turned away to have a private conversation. After she was done, she looked back at me sheepishly and said, "I'm really flattered, but I have to go."

"Eddie, put it on my tab." She downed the remainder of her drink and stood to leave.

"It's on the house. This is the best laugh I had all month." She eyed him and smirked, shaking her head as she headed to the door.

I sat at the bar in shock. As I watched her leave, I felt embarrassed and stupid. It seemed like the walls of the bar were closing in on me making the room seem even more rank and depressing. The few people in the place turned their attention away from me and back to their previous conversations.

"Hey, we all make mistakes," Eddie piped up. "Don't let it get you down."

"Ah, I'm okay. I just wish I wasn't so gullible." I went to pick up the flowers from the bar, then paused. "These are for you, Eddie."

"You're so sweeeeeet!" He joked, trying make his deep voice more feminine. "Try not to be, and you'll do better next time."

The businessman pulled himself back up to the bar. He looked at me, snorted, and returned to laughing uncontrollably. It was definitely time to leave.

I walked out of the bar and got into my car. Looking into the rearview mirror all I could see was roses. Great. Just great. There had to be a silver lining somewhere in these rosy clouds.

On my way home I passed by a church and decided to stop. Maybe it was my Catholic upbringing. I thought it would be appropriate to leave my bounty of bouquets there. A cleaning crew was preparing the church for service. Nobody thought to ask why I was delivering flowers. It was a common occurrence for a church to receive flowers, except the florist usually arrives in a van.

After I finished, the minister stopped me. He was a spritely, bald man with light blue eyes and a grey goatee. "What beautiful flowers! Are we having a wedding?" He asked enthusiastically.

"No," I replied.

"Sunday service?" he asked, puzzled.

"Nope," I replied.

His demeanor changed quickly and he asked in a hushed tone, "Did someone...transition?"

"Well, sort of." The minister looked at me surprised. Not knowing how to explain my situation, I started to backpedal. He placed his gentle hand on my shoulder as if to comfort me. I could tell he had years of experience counseling people, but I doubt he would understand my plight.

"No, no, no. Consider it a donation."

The minister was relieved, although a little confused, "Thank you, my son. They will be thoroughly enjoyed by all."

As I walked out of the church, I realized why I may have

unconsciously selected this location as the resting place for my

gift. The marquee for Sunday service read:

A WOMAN MISUNDERSTOOD

A TRIBUTE TO MARY MAGDELENE

Chapter 10: The Eternal Sunshine of a Spotless Mind

There you have it, the worst Internet dates of my life. Well, currently that's true. You may have had similar luck in finding love online. Any date can turn out to be funny, or scary, or really sad. You never know what you might get with the many types of people in the world. We are all inherently flawed, but search for companionship in the hope that someone else finds our quirky behavior endearing. The road to a great relationship is never smooth, and although we do our best to stay on the map, there are always detours along the way. The best we can do is enjoy the ride.

THE END

Good luck to you and thank you for purchasing this book! If you want to be informed of my upcoming projects, visit my website at chrismastersbooks.com.

www.ingramcontent.com/pod-product-compliance
Lightning Source LLC
Chambersburg PA
CBHW060511030426
42337CB00015B/1848